⌒972   Bulmer-Thomas,
              Barbara.

              Journey through
              Mexico.

$12.50

DATE			

JOURNEY THROUGH

Mexico

Barbara Bulmer-Thomas

Troll Associates

Library of Congress Cataloging-in-Publication Data

Bulmer-Thomas, Barbara.
    Journey through Mexico / by Barbara
Bulmer-Thomas; illustrated by Martin
Camm...[et al.].
        p.   cm.
    Summary: Describes the geography, sights,
and prominent places of Mexico. Includes
a chart of key facts and information on the
population, religion, and festivals.
    ISBN 0-8167-2116-5 (lib. bdg.)
    ISBN 0-8167-2117-3 (pbk.)
    1. Mexico—Juvenile literature.
[1. Mexico.]   I. Camm, Martin, ill.
II. Title.
F1208.5.B85   1991
972—dc20   90-10950

Published by Troll Associates, Mahwah,
New Jersey 07430

Edited by Neil Morris

Design by James Marks
Picture research by Caroline Mitchell.

Illustrators: Martin Camm: pages 4, 5, 15, 21;
Robina Green pages 22-23, 24-25; Mike Roffe:
pages 5, 10-11; Paul Sullivan: page 7;
Ian Thompson: pages 4-5.

Picture Credits: J Allan Cash: page 13 (left);
Geoscience Features: page 25; Robert Harding:
page 14; Hutchison: pages 6-7 (top), 9, 27;
Mexicolore: pages 26-27; Popperphoto page 21;
South American Pics pages 6-7 (bottom), 8-9 (top &
bottom), 10, 11, 12-13, 13 (right), 15, 18-19, 19, 23
ZEFA: cover, pages 1,16, 17, 18, 20-21, 22 (top &
bottom), 28, 29, 30.
Printed in the U.S.A.
10   9   8   7   6   5   4   3   2   1

CONTENTS

Mexico

● Tijuana

Gulf of California

BAJA CALIFORNIA

SONORA

Sierra Madre Occidental

● Cananea

● Chihuahua

● Los Mochis

Río Bravo (Río Grande)

Sierra Madre Oriental

Monterrey ●

● Durango

Cabo San Lucas

P A C I F I C

● Zacatecas

G U L F

O F

Animals of Mexico
Armadillos and iguanas live in Mexico. The armadillo has hard plates over its back and sides. The iguana is a large lizard that lives in the rain forest.

● Puerto Vallarta

León ●
Guadalajara ●

Lake Chapala

Teotihuacán ● ● Pachuca

MEXICO CITY ■

Ixtacíhuatl ▲ **Puebla** ▲ ● Veracruz
Popocatépetl ▲ Citlaltépetl (Pico de Orizaba)

Sierra Madre del Sur

TABASCO

● Acapulco
Oaxaca ●
San Cristóbal de las Casas ●

O A X A C A

C H I A

Gulf of Tehuantepec

● Tapachula

O C E A N

Iguana

4

14-15

20-21

18-19

16-17

8-13

◀ In this book, we will take a journey through Mexico. The numbers on the small map show which pages deal with which part of Mexico.

The Mexican flag has green, white, and red vertical stripes, with the national emblem of the eagle, snake, and cactus. The Mexican national anthem is the *Himno Nacional*, composed by Bocanegra in the 19th century.

Armadillo

22-23 24-25 26-27

M E X I C O

Cancún
Chichén Itzá
YUCATÁN
Uxmal
YUCATÁN PENINSULA
QUINTANA
CAMPECHE   ROO
Rio Hondo
Palenque
Rio Usumacinta
P A S

KEY FACTS

Area: 1,967,000 sq. km (761,500 sq. mi.)

Population: 88,087,000 – largest Spanish-speaking population anywhere in the world

Capital: Mexico City, more than 16,000,000 people

Other major cities: Guadalajara 2,245,000 Monterrey 1,916,000 Puebla 836,000

Highest mountain: Citlaltépetl (Pico de Orizaba) 5,699 m (18,698 ft.)

Longest rivers: Rio Bravo (also called Rio Grande) 3,030 km (1,885 mi.)
Rio Lerma Santiago 1,010 km (628 mi.)

Largest lake: Lake Chapala 1,080 sq.km (417 sq. mi.)

Welcome to Mexico

Mexico is a country of beautiful contrasts. You can travel by plane, flying over snow-capped mountains to hot, tropical coastlines. You can take a bus or train from dusty deserts in the north to lush rain forests in the south.

Most Mexicans are *mestizos*, people of Indian and Spanish ancestry. Mexicans are proud of their Indian heritage. Indian tribes lived here for thousands of years before Europeans first arrived. Spain conquered Mexico less than 500 years ago.

Many Indians still speak their own languages. But like everyone else in Mexico, they speak Spanish as well. Some Indian words have become part of the Spanish and English languages. Many are the names of foods that were first discovered in Mexico, such as tomato, avocado, and chocolate.

The Sierra Madre mountain chains run like twin backbones down the length of Mexico. Some of these mountains are active volcanoes, and between them are high plateaus. Altitude governs the weather – the higher you are, the cooler it is. Most of Mexico's large towns lie on a high central plateau.

It is over 4,000 kilometers (2,500 miles) by road from Tijuana, on the northern border, to the southern town of Tapachula. At the airport, bus or railway station, people pay for their tickets in *pesos*, Mexican money.

► Mexico is a country of mountain chains and volcanoes. The snowcapped Nevado de Toluca is about 4,577 meters (15,017 feet) high. This extinct volcano is part of Mexico's highest mountain range.

▲ Easter celebrations in a Mexican street. Festivals are very important in Mexico. Lively pageants may go on for days. They often blend the country's Christian and Indian traditions.

▶ The Zinacantecos live in the southern state of Chiapas. They wear striped woolen *serapes*, or shawls, and short trousers.

Mexico's capital city

Mexico City is the country's capital. Most foreign visitors arrive at the busy airport, on direct flights from the United States of America or elsewhere.

This is the most crowded and fastest-growing city in the world. More than 16 million people live in the Mexico City area. It is thought that by the year 2000 there will be over 30 million. The city lies at a height of 2,240 meters (7,349 feet), which means that the air is thin. Visitors need time to get used to this, especially as the air is also made dirty by fumes churned out by industry and millions of cars. The surrounding mountains help to trap the fumes and cause a blanket of smog.

Mexico City is full of strong contrasts. You can see beautiful old Spanish-style buildings next to space-age skyscrapers. Colorful open-air markets bustle with life, around the corner from department stores covering several blocks. You can also still see evidence of the terrible earthquake of 1985. This left whole areas of the city in ruins.

One in every five Mexicans lives in the capital city. Many have modern apartments, and families stay close together. Most young people live with their parents until they get married. Children go to primary school when they are six. School usually starts at 8:00 in the morning and finishes at 1:00 in the afternoon.

Soccer is the most popular sport in Mexico. Bullfights are still common too. The giant bullring in Mexico City is the largest in the world. It seats about 50,000 people.

▶ Mexico City is often covered by a blanket of smog. The 1985 earthquake caused great damage.

◄ Mexican children have a Christmas party that includes the *piñata*. This is a papier-mâché figure of an animal or a person, filled with candy and toys. The piñata swings from the ceiling. A child is blindfolded, given a stick, and has three chances to hit the piñata and break it.

▼ The giant bullring in Mexico City. For many Mexican people, bullfighting is not a sport. They believe it is an art, in which the bullfighters pit their courage and skill against the bulls.

The eagle and the snake

You can take a bus or subway to the center of Mexico City. The great city began here over 600 years ago. A wandering tribe of Indians, the Aztecs, were looking for a home. According to Indian legend, their high priest told them that they must build a city where they found an eagle perched on a cactus eating a snake. In 1325 they at last saw the eagle they were looking for, on an island in the middle of a lake.

Here the Aztecs built the capital of a great empire. They called it Tenochtitlán, and this became the modern-day Mexico City. The eagle and the snake form the symbol on the Mexican flag. They are also remembered on banknotes, coins, and woven designs all over Mexico.

▼ The temples of Tenochtitlán, the Aztec capital, once looked like this. Mexico City was built on top of Tenochtitlán.

◀ The library of the University of Mexico. It is covered with a *mural*, or wall painting, by the artist Juan O'Gorman.

Almost 200 years later, a visitor from faraway Spain arrived, wearing armor and riding a horse. His name was Hernán Cortés. Montezuma, the Aztec emperor, had never seen a horse before. He received Cortés as an honored guest. But Spanish soldiers took Montezuma prisoner and smashed the Aztec city to the ground. Cortés built a new Spanish empire. Spanish rule lasted until 1821, when Mexico won its independence.

Some Aztec remains were only found in recent years when the subway was built. So as you wait for your underground train at Montezuma station, you can think of the great events of the city's past. But don't dream too long. There is a great crush in the rush hour. Some of the busiest subway stations even make separate entries for women and children. These are patrolled by armed guards to protect people from the crush!

▲ The Cathedral, Mexico City, stands on the huge Zócalo, one of the largest public squares in the world.

Smoking Mountain and White Lady

On a clear day you can see the snow-capped peaks of two volcanoes from Mexico City center. These are Popocatépetl (Indian for "Smoking Mountain"), 5,452 meters (17,887 feet) high, and Ixtacíhuatl ("White Lady"), 5,286 meters (17,342 feet). Popo's last major eruption was in 1802, and both volcanoes are dormant.

To climb the volcanoes, you can take a bus to the National Park that surrounds them. If the weather is good and you are properly equipped, you can climb to the rim of Popo's crater. It was here that Cortés lowered some of his men down to gather sulfur for gunpowder.

It is a day-long expedition, and your Mexican guide will tell you the legend of the mountains. Popocatépetl was a warrior, and Ixtacíhuatl was the Aztec emperor's beautiful daughter. Ixta thought Popo had been killed, and she died of grief. When Popo returned alive, he laid her body down on the mountain. He then stood guard over her, holding a burning torch. He is the Smoking Mountain, and she is the White Lady.

From Mexico City, you can catch a bus north to Pachuca. This old town nestles in the mountainside. It is important because it has something both beautiful and very valuable – silver. It was here that the Aztecs first dug the mines that were later taken over by the Spanish. Pachuca, with its steep winding lanes and small public squares called *plazas*, still has the biggest silver mine in the world.

The mountains of Mexico are rich in other metals and minerals too. There is zinc, lead, mercury, and the most prized of them all – gold.

▲ The two volcanoes, Popocatépetl and Ixtacíhuatl. Popo sometimes sends up a spiral of steam, but the volcanoes have not erupted for a long time.

▶ A silversmith at work. Pure silver is soft and easy to shape. It is the whitest of all metals, and is very popular for use as jewelry.

▲ The Pyramid of the Sun at the pre-Aztec site, Teotihuacán.

13

The United States border

If you take a plane from Mexico City to the very north of the country, you will fly over the western Sierra Madre range of mountains and the Gulf of California. One of the most famous northern towns is Tijuana, near the U.S.A., where millions of people cross the border every year.

Much of what is now the U.S.A., including the states of Texas, Arizona, and California, once belonged to Mexico. The U.S.A. claimed them after winning a war with Mexico in 1848.

▶ Corn is one of Mexico's main crops, along with wheat and cotton. Farmers cut and harvest a crop of corn.

▼ The town of Cananea is in Sonora, just south of the U.S. border. Here, industry is surrounded by a very bare landscape.

▼ A mother gray whale with her calf. In spring the whales return from Baja California to their summer feeding grounds in the Arctic seas.

To the east of Tijuana, the Gran Desierto – Great Desert – stretches for 200 kilometers (125 miles) along the border with Arizona. Seemingly endless sand dunes and volcanic hills make the landscape look like the barren surface of the moon. In contrast, the south of the state of Sonora is rich farming land, with vast wheat fields.

Highway 1 runs from Tijuana all the way down the peninsula of Baja California. The highway passes Guerrero Negro, a small town with a modern desalination plant – a factory for getting salt from the sea. Here you can also watch gray whales in their breeding grounds. These whales are among the largest mammals in the world. They make an 8,000-kilometer (5,000-mile) journey from Alaska to Mexico every year. Their young are born and reared under the protection of their mothers in the bays and lagoons along the peninsula's rugged coast. There are organized trips to watch the whales without disturbing them.

Horsemen and high divers

The ferry from Cabo San Lucas takes you across Pacific waters to Puerto Vallarta. From here you can take a bus across country to Guadalajara, Mexico's second largest city.

Mexico is a great cattle-raising country, and a favorite pastime is the *charreada*, the Mexican version of the rodeo. Guadalajara is famous for its rodeos. This is a chance for horsemen to show off their skills. Wearing embroidered costumes and wide-brimmed hats called *sombreros*, the cowboys gallop into the ring on their horses. At full speed, they ride alongside an unsaddled wild horse called a *bronco*. The cowboys try to jump onto the bronco's back and ride it, holding onto its mane.

From Guadalajara you can take a train or a plane to one of the most famous beach resorts in the world – Acapulco. This was an important port in Spanish colonial times. Today people flock there to enjoy the beautiful beaches, sunshine, and warm blue sea.

▶ Acapulco's famous divers at La Quebrada plunge from the cliffs into a rocky channel of water. Their dive must coincide with an incoming wave, because there must be enough water to stop them from hitting the bottom. The divers also must get out of the sea without being dashed against the rocks.

▶ Mexicans are great horse lovers, and Mexico is well known for its crossbred horses. Horses that Spanish explorers left behind in Mexico were probably the ancestors of American wild horses. Cowboys sometimes wear leather *chaps* over their trousers. These protect the legs from thorny brush, and from rubbing during long hours in the saddle.

On the slopes of the Sierra Madre

Heading back up north, road or rail will take you to Zacatecas. With its old buildings and cobbled lanes, this is a beautiful town. It lies at 2,496 meters (8,189 feet), high up in the western Sierra Madre mountain range. The Spanish founded the town in 1546 and discovered silver in the surrounding mountains.

Continuing north, you come to Durango, an important industrial center. Movie fans will want to visit the area outside town where many westerns have been filmed. But on any trips, watch out for scorpions. A type of white scorpion lives here, and its sting can be deadly.

In all these country towns, the main plaza, or public square, is the center of business and social life. The town's important buildings, shops, and

▲ The main plaza of Mexican towns is a lively meeting place. A town's most important buildings are usually around the plaza.

◀ A *mariachi* band, with trumpet, guitars, and violins. You can hear rhythmic mariachi music in the streets and plazas throughout Mexico.

▶ *Tortillas* served with meat and sausage. These corn pancakes are eaten plain, fried, or toasted. They usually make up one course of a large meal in a restaurant.

restaurants are usually around the plaza. People meet there to chat, eat, and drink. But many places close in the afternoon between two and five o'clock. This is *siesta* time, when people take a rest or nap during the hottest part of the day.

When you eat at restaurants in Mexico, you will find that meals are quite large. They consist of a series of different courses. One of the most common foods is the *tortilla*, a thin corn pancake. It is often served with a filling of meat, vegetables, cheese, and spices. For a poor Mexican family at home, tortillas and *frijoles* (beans) might be a complete meal.

A popular dish for festivals is *mole poblano*, which is made from an old Indian recipe. It contains lots of ingredients, including hot spices and chocolate.

The Copper Canyon Railway

If you head across the Sierra Madre mountains to the Pacific coast, you can make a 13-hour train journey that you will never forget. The Copper Canyon Railway starts at Los Mochis near the coast, crosses vast canyons and high peaks, and finally arrives on the plains of Chihuahua.

The line goes through 90 tunnels, over 30 bridges and climbs to 2,480 meters (8,140 feet). Through your window you will see an amazing variety of scenery, beginning with groves of palms and bamboos, then rocks and gorges, hills covered with pine forests, and at last plateaus with nothing but cactus plants. The *Barranca del Cobre* (Copper Canyon) is a series of huge gorges, 1,200 meters (3,900 feet) deep and 1,500 meters (4,900 feet) across. You may even catch sight of some Tarahumara Indians, who live in small groups in this area.

Chihuahua was the home of Francisco "Pancho" Villa, a popular bandit leader of the Mexican Revolution of 1910-17. Leaders like Villa and Emiliano Zapata struggled to help people who had no land and were short of food. The revolution cost the lives of thousands of Mexicans. But it won many rights for the country's peasant farmers and industrial workers.

You can go on by rail to the industrial city of Monterrey. This is the heart of the country's iron and steel industry. The steel produced here is raw material for the factories nearby. These factories make cars, refrigerators, washing machines, and other goods. From here it is only 150 kilometers (90 miles) to the Rio Bravo del Norte, also known as the Rio Grande, the great river that forms the border between Mexico and Texas, U.S.A.

▲ Francisco "Pancho" Villa (1877-1923) was a bandit leader of the Mexican Revolution. He was finally shot dead on his own ranch.

▲ The chihuahua is the smallest breed of dog. It was named after the Mexican state.

◀ Crossing one of the bridges of Copper Canyon. Mexico has 25,800 kilometers (16,000 miles) of railway.

The Gulf of Mexico

The old town of Veracruz, Mexico's main port, can be reached by sea, air, road, or rail. Between about 1200 and 400 B.C., the Olmec Indians lived in this area. Nearby are ruins of temples and pyramids built by the later Totonac Indians. Veracruz was the first town founded by the Spanish in Mexico, in 1519.

It lies in the heart of oil-producing country. Many refineries and other industries operate here. The large harbor is ideal for shipping. Mexico is the fourth biggest producer of oil in the world. When oil prices were high, foreign banks and governments were willing to lend big sums of money to the Mexican government. But when oil prices fell, Mexico had difficulty paying the money back.

▲ An oil rig in the Gulf of Mexico. Vast oil reserves were discovered here in the 1970s.

◀ Workers on a drilling platform in Tabasco. The drill bit that bores into the earth soon becomes blunt. The men who handle the drill equipment are called "roughnecks."

▶ The "dance of the flying men" is an amazing ceremony still performed by the Totonac Indians.

The Totonac Indians have kept alive the amazing ceremony of the diving dancers. Five men climb to a small platform at the top of a tall pole. While one plays music, the others launch themselves off the platform. They have ropes tied around their bodies and to their feet, attached to the top of the pole. They swing down, head first, circling around as the ropes unwind until they reach the ground. Quite a feat!

The neighboring state of Tabasco is a flat region with lakes, rivers, swamps, and dense rain forest. Many species of tropical animals live here, including crocodiles. The main commercial crops are bananas, coconut palms, cacao, coffee, and sugar cane.

▲ A monumental stone head carved by Olmec Indians, perhaps as long ago as 1000 B.C. The head is 2.4 meters (almost 8 feet) high. The Olmec were also skilled at carving jade.

Land of the Maya

The states of Campeche, Yucatán, and Quintana Roo make up the Yucatán peninsula. The journey along the coast road to Campeche involves a series of ferry rides across wide river mouths and lagoons.

The peninsula is a flat, low-lying plain. It is blisteringly hot and humid. Large parts are covered by tropical rain forests. Until 30 years ago when proper roads and railways were built, it was almost as if the Yucatán was separate from the rest of Mexico. Yet this was an area of very early civilization. This is the land of the Maya.

Mayan Indians settled in the Yucatán by 800 B.C. They lived in huts similar to those you can still see in the villages today. Many tourists come to the great Mayan ruins at Chichén Itzá, Uxmal, and Palenque in Chiapas. You can see impressive pyramids, temples, palaces, and tombs.

The Maya had an observatory for looking at the stars and planets. The Mayan calendar was much more complicated than our own. It divided the 365-day year into 18 months. Over a thousand years ago, the Mayan empire spread over most of Central America. It is still a mystery why this great empire suddenly collapsed around 900 A.D.

Yucatán's plants are very important. The sisal plant has strong fibers which are used to make rope. Over half the world's sisal comes from here. Sapodilla trees are tapped for a sticky substance called *chicle*. This is sent to factories to be purified and made into chewing gum.

▶ The Temple of the Warriors at Chichén Itzá, a great Mayan site in Yucatán. The temple is on a terraced platform. Chichén Itzá was probably founded by Mayan tribes about A.D. 450.

▶ The Mayan people played a sacred game on ball courts. Players tried to hit a rubber ball through a stone ring with their elbows or hips. A ball court was discovered next to the Temple of the Warriors at Chichén Itzá (*above*).

The southern states

The Rio Hondo river forms the border between Mexico and the small country of Belize. Further west, the Rio Usumacinta flows through dense rain forest and forms part of the border with Guatemala. If you go even further west, you pass through the state of Chiapas to Oaxaca.

Oaxaca is one of the most varied Mexican states. It has long stretches of beach on the Pacific coast. The rugged mountains of the southern Sierra Madre have forests and deep valleys. And there is vast open land covered with scrub and cactuses. Oaxaca is rich in minerals, such as silver, gold, coal, uranium, and onyx, yet it is one of the poorer Mexican states.

This is Mixtec and Zapotec Indian country. The most famous Zapotec was Benito Juárez. He came from a poor peasant family, and rose to become President of Mexico in 1858. His term as president was interrupted for four years when the French invaded Mexico and made Austrian Archduke Maximilian emperor of Mexico.

The town of Oaxaca has not suffered from too much industry or too many people. Many music and dance festivals are held here. Bustling markets sell traditional crafts, such as handwoven blankets and shawls, all in rich, clashing colors.

Indians first inhabited the Oaxaca valley about 6,000 years ago. The Spanish arrived in the 1500s. There are still 17 different Indian peoples living in the many little towns.

All Mexicans are proud of their past, but they also make up a nation that looks forward to the future. Our journey through Mexico has shown us great contrasts. Indian pyramids and temples, great mountains and volcanoes, the skyscrapers of Mexico City – all are part of modern Mexico.

▲ Black glazed pottery and other wares on sale in Oaxaca market. Oaxaca is well known for woven articles, basketwork, glass, carved wood, and leather goods.

◄ People from surrounding villages gather in the markets of Chiapas and Oaxaca. Their colorful costumes vary from village to village.

Fact file

United Mexican States

Mexico is a federal republic, made up of 31 states and the Federal District of Mexico City. The head of the state is the President, who is elected for six years and can never be re-elected. The President chooses his own council of Ministers. Each state has an elected governor.

Population

2.5 million babies are born in Mexico every year. Mexico is a country of young people. Half of the population is under 20 years of age. This has created a problem of unemployment. Many young people try to find jobs in the U.S.A. when they leave school.

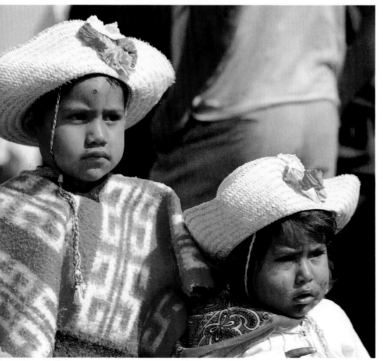

Approximately 60 per cent of the Mexican people are *mestizos*, whose ancestors were Indians and Europeans. About 25 per cent are Indians, and about 15 per cent are of European, Asian, and African descent.

Religion

Most people (93 per cent) are Roman Catholics.

Mexican money

The unit of currency is the *peso*, which is made up of 100 *centavos*.

Time zones

Mexico is divided into four time zones, each one hour behind the other. The Yucatán peninsula has Eastern Time; the central zone has Central Time; the western area has Mountain Time; and Baja California Norte has Pacific Time. If you travel from east to west, you can gain an hour with each new zone!

Coastline

Mexico has almost 10,000 km (6,200 mi.) of coastline: 7,150 km (4,440 mi.) on the Pacific Ocean, and 2,760 km (1,720 mi.) on the Atlantic Ocean. There are many small islands off both coasts.

◄ Young children in traditional dress. In Mexico, there are over 50 Indian languages. Many children only learn Spanish when they go to school.

Farming

Because of Mexico's dry climate and rugged mountains, only a small amount of the land can be used for farming. The main crops are cotton, coffee, fruit, wheat, sorghum, corn, sugar cane, and vegetables. Mexico is the world's tenth largest producer of meat. Cattle are raised in the dry areas of the north, and sheep graze on the Central Plateau. The most rugged areas are suitable only for goats.

Owning the land

Before the Revolution, Mexico had huge farming estates called *haciendas*. These were owned by a few very rich people. Since then, new laws have created a new farming system. Now the state owns the land, and divides it up into small farms. Farming families feed themselves and sell extra crops at market for profit.

Wall painting

One of the greatest Mexican arts is *mural* (wall) painting. Before the Spanish conquest, murals were a beautiful art of the Mayan culture. Magnificent examples can be seen in many Mayan temples. The art has been revived in this century. One of the most famous Mexican muralists was Diego Rivera (1886-1957). Influenced by the Aztecs and the Maya, Rivera painted many huge murals in public buildings, mostly in Mexico City. The paintings tell of Mexican history, politics, and society.

Beans

Mexico has more varieties of beans than any other country – about 50 different kinds. Beans are used in one of the most famous Mexican dishes, *chile con carne* ("chili with meat"). This is a spicy dish of meat, beans, chilies, onions, and other spices.

The language of Mexico

When the Spanish conquered Mexico, they brought their language with them. Now the Mexicans speak Spanish. Say it in Spanish!

hello	hola
goodbye	adiós
please	por favor
thank you	gracias

▲ A theater with a Diego Rivera mural.

Folk music

Mexican folk musicians play trumpets, guitars, violins, harps, and *marimbas* (sets of wooden plates played with soft hammers, similar to xylophones). Everywhere you hear *mariachi* bands, made up of trumpeters, guitarists, violinists, and a singer. Their music is brisk and rhythmic, and they play in the streets and plazas.

Festivals

Every town and village in Mexico has a *fiesta* (festival) in honor of the local patron saint. There are many other celebrations, including the main church festivals and national holidays. Many fiestas combine old Indian rituals with Christian practices. Some of the main festivals are:

February 5th	Constitution Day (remembering 1917)
March 21st	Birthday of Benito Juárez (1806)
September 16th	Independence Day (1810)
November 2nd	Day of the Dead – an Aztec festival when Mexicans remember their dead friends and relatives
November 20th	Revolution Day (1910)
December 16th -24th	*Posadas* – a Christian festival remembering Mary and Joseph's journey to Bethlehem
December 25th	*Navidad* – Christmas Day

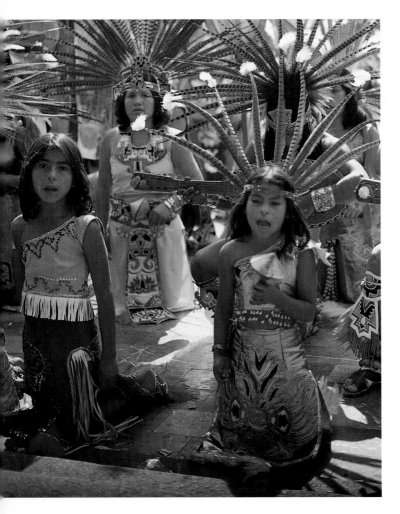

◄ On December 12th, people from all over Mexico visit the Basilica of Our Lady of Guadalupe. On this day they honor the nation's patron saint. Much of the pageant is in the Indian style.

B.C.	Time chart	1861	French troops land at Veracruz.
10,000-5000	Primitive nomadic peoples hunt and gather food.	1864	Archduke Maximilian von Hapsburg becomes Emperor of Mexico.
1500	Settled farming communities, growing corn, beans, and squashes. Trade between communities develops.	1867	French troops leave. Maximilian is executed. Juárez is reinstated as President.
1200-400	Olmecs settle in Oaxaca Valley, and develop a calendar and primitive writing.	1876-1911	Dictatorship of Porfirio Díaz.
c 800	Mayan culture first appears.	1890s	Oil found off Tampico.
A.D.		1910	Mexican Revolution begins.
600	Mixtecs write earliest book on the American continent, on deerskin.	1917	Congress makes a new constitution.
900	Decline of Mayan cities.	1920s	The Roman Catholic Church fights the government and loses property and power.
1200-1521	The Aztec Empire.	1929	The National Revolutionary Party is founded, bringing together Mexico's most important political forces.
1325	Aztecs found their capital Tenochtitlán.		
1502-1520	Montezuma is ruler of the Aztecs.	1931	Mexico joins the League of Nations.
1519	Hernán Cortés founds Veracruz.	1938	President Lázaro Cárdenas nationalizes oil companies previously owned by British and U.S. interests.
1521	Cortés defeats Aztecs.		
1526	Dominican monks arrive to convert the Indians to Roman Catholicism. Many monasteries and churches are built.	1942	War declared against Germany.
		1943	Social Security established.
1535	Mexico is made a Spanish Viceroyalty, part of New Spain.	1953	Women get the vote.
1551	University of Mexico founded.	1968	Summer Olympic Games held in Mexico City.
1808-1821	Mexico fights for independence from Spain.	1970	Soccer World Cup finals in Mexico.
1824	Mexico is declared a republic.		
1845	The U.S.A. annexes Texas.	1985	Earthquake devastates large parts of Mexico City.
1848	Border war with U.S.A. ends. Mexico loses several states, including California.	1986	Soccer World Cup finals in Mexico.
1857-1860	Civil war. Benito Juárez becomes President.	1988	Hurricane Gilbert wrecks Cancún, an island resort in Quintana Roo.

Index